D1089151

Speed Racer
Kids with Attention-Deficit/Hyperactivity Disorder

Kids with Special Needs

Speed Racer
Kids with Attention-Deficit/ Hyperactivity Disorder

by Sheila Stewart and Camden Flath

MASON CREST PUBLISHERS INC.
370 Reed Road
Broomall, Pennsylvania 19008
(866)MCP-BOOK (toll free)
www.masoncrest.com

First Printing
9 8 7 6 5 4 3 2 1

ISBN (set) 978-1-4222-1727-6   ISBN (pbk set) 978-1-4222-1918-8

Library of Congress Cataloging-in-Publication Data

Stewart, Sheila, 1975–
  Speed racer : kids with attention-deficit/hyperactivity disorder / by Sheila Stewart and Camden Flath.
      p. cm.
  ISBN 978-1-4222-1721-4   ISBN (pbk) 978-1-4222-1924-9
  1. Attention-deficit/hyperactivity disorder—Juvenile literature. I. Flath, Camden, 1987– II. Title.
  RJ506.H9S734 2010
  618.92'8589—dc22
                              2010004981

Produced by Harding House Publishing Service, Inc.
www.hardinghousepages.com
Design by MK Bassett-Harvey.
Cover design by Torque Advertising Design.
Printed in the USA by Bang Printing.

Photo Credits

Creative Commons Attribution 2.0 Generic pg 34; Dreamstime: Aaronamat Pg 39; Armyagov, Andrey Pg 27; Cunningham, Sandra Pg 36; Monkeybusinessimages Pg 29; Raths, Alexander Pg 33; Ron Chapple Studios Pg 40; Showface Pg 30; Tucker, Suzanne Pg 26; Voronin76 Pg 38.

Introduction

To the Teacher

Kids with Special Needs provides a unique forum for demystifying a wide variety of childhood medical and developmental disabilities. Written to captivate an elementary-level audience, the books bring to life the challenges and triumphs experienced by children with common chronic conditions such as hearing loss, intellectual disability, physical differences, and speech difficulties. The topics are addressed frankly through a blend of fiction and fact.

This series is particularly important today as the number of children with special needs is on the rise. Over the last two decades, advances in pediatric medical techniques have allowed children who have chronic illnesses and disabilities to live longer, more functional lives. At the same time, IDEA, a federal law, guarantees their rights to equal educational opportunities. As a result, these children represent an increasingly visible part of North American population in all aspects of daily life. Students are exposed to peers with special needs in their classrooms, through extracurricular activities, and in the community. Often, young people have misperceptions and unanswered questions about a child's disabilities—and more important, his or her abilities. Many times, there is no vehicle for talking about these complex issues in a comfortable manner.

This series will encourage further conversation about these issues. Most important, the series promotes a greater comfort for its readers as they live, play, and study side by side with these children who have medical and developmental differences—kids with special needs.

—*Dr. Carolyn Bridgemohan*
Boston Pediatric Hospital/Harvard Medical School

"Jay Jay."

I didn't even hear Mrs. Harris say my name. She'd been talking about the rainforest, and that was where I lost her. I started drawing a dark jungle, with a panther hiding in a tree, getting ready to leap on an unsuspecting explorer. My knees were jiggling like crazy—like they usually do. I growled in the back of my throat like the panther would be doing.

"Jay Jay!"

Mrs. Harris was standing right next to my desk, staring down at the drawing. I looked around; everyone else in class was staring at me. Somebody giggled.

I felt my face get hot. I hated people laughing at me.

"Jay Jay, I asked you a question," Mrs. Harris said. "Do you know what it was?"

Of course I didn't know what it was. I hadn't heard a thing she'd said for at least five minutes. And Mrs. Harris knew that, too.

She reached down and started to take the drawing off my desk. I didn't want her to, so I put my hand on it and tried to hold it down. She pulled harder and the corner of the paper ripped.

Just like that, I got really, really mad. I stood up and yelled, "Give me back my paper!"

Of course, I got sent to the principal's office. My mom and I moved here a month ago and I've already been sent to the principal's office three times. I think Mrs. Harris hates me.

I ran down the hall, kind of banging against the walls and then bouncing off again as I went. A teacher opened a door and yelled at me to stop running, but I just kept going.

Mr. Martinez shook his head when I walked into his office.

"Sit down, Jay Jay," he said. "Tell me what happened this time."

I flopped down in the chair by his desk, but I couldn't sit still. I got up again and picked up a model airplane that was on the desk. I made it take off and then zoomed it around a bit. For a minute, I really did forget that I was supposed to be telling Mr. Martinez what had happened with Mrs. Harris.

"Jay Jay!" Mr. Martinez's voice was louder than usual. "Sit down!"

And then he said the worst possible thing.

"Jay Jay, I think we're going to have to call your mother."

Mom looked really worried when she walked into Mr. Martinez's office. She had come straight from the theater downtown where she worked designing costumes, and she had both a paintbrush and a pencil sticking out of her ponytail.

As soon as I saw her, I felt tears coming up in my eyes, partly because I love her so much and partly because I felt really bad I'd gotten into trouble and made her come to the school. I couldn't believe I was crying! I'm ten years old!

I turned my back on Mom so she wouldn't see I was crying and started kicking Mr. Martinez's book-shelves.

Mom put her hand on my shoulder in a way that was almost like a hug. "What hap-pened?" she asked. I couldn't tell whether she was asking Mr. Martinez or me, but I didn't answer and just kicked the bookshelf harder.

Mr. Martinez told Mom what had happened—Mrs. Harris had come in and told him all about it while we were waiting for Mom. Then he said, "Ms. Rowan, I think Jay Jay needs further evaluation."

Mom didn't say anything for a minute, and then she asked, "What kind of evaluation?"

"He should be tested for ADHD," Mr. Martinez said.

ADHD sounded like something I might have heard before, but I had no idea what the letters meant. It sounded scary though.

In our apartment that night, Mom told me that ADHD means attention-deficit hyperactivity disorder. She said it was when people have trouble paying attention to one thing at a time or sitting still, because their minds are always jumping from one thing to another. She'd been reading about it on the Internet. We both agreed that it did sound like me.

"So I guess that might explain why I'm so stupid and awful." I felt kind of relieved to think their might be an answer, that I was just a bad kid.

Mom put her face really close to mine and stared me right in the eyes. "Don't you ever say that again," she said. "You are not stupid. You are not awful. You are amazing and wonderful and you are not allowed to ever forget that."

Two weeks later, Mom and I went to see a child psychiatrist. Dr. Kelley. I was scared, but she was really nice, so I started to relax. She talked to me for a long time, and to Mom, too. It was mostly a lot of talking, but Dr. Kelley did play some games with me that were kind of fun.

And at the end of it, it came down to this: Yes, I did have ADHD.

The first thing Dr. Kelley wanted Mom and I do was get organized. This was really hard for both of us. Mom isn't an organized person and she hates having to do things in a certain way.

We made a schedule of all the things we had to do every day and put it on the fridge. Mom made it pretty by drawing trees and birds and animals on it. That made her feel a little better about it, but I still wasn't sure. I was used to coming home from school, getting something to eat, watching some TV, maybe seeing if spreading butter on the floor made my cars go faster (it didn't), whatever. The point is, I didn't really think about what I was going to do; I just did it. Mom always made me do my homework sometime before bed. That was a pain for both of us, because I didn't want to do it and she hated having to make me but she knew she had to.

But now, there was the schedule, and I was supposed to think about what I was going to do next. It said things like:

3:45 p.m.—Home from school. Have a snack.

4:00 p.m.—Homework. Make sure Mom checks it.

5:00 p.m.—Help Mom make supper. Set the table.

And so on.

It sucked all the fun out of life, if you asked me.

The next Monday in school, Mrs. Harris told us, "The Science Fair is coming up in two months. Each of you is going to do a project. The project can be an experiment or an invention. You will come up with an idea, keep a science journal about your project, make the display, and do all the work yourself. It will be a lot of work, but it should also be a lot of fun."

It did kind of sound fun. I loved doing experiments. I started getting excited. I raised my hand and started waving it around, so Mrs. Harris would be sure to see it.

I could tell she did see me, because she looked at me and sighed, but she answered a question one of the girls was asking before she finally said, "Yes, Jay Jay? What is it?"

"Can the project be about whatever we want?" I asked.

"Within reason," Mrs. Harris said.

"What does that mean?" I asked. "Can I do an experiment to see which foods stick to the ceiling the best? Or an experiment about whether you can really break glass by screaming?"

"Your experiment should not be dangerous or destructive in any way," Mrs. Harris said. "It should teach you something about science and it should not make more work for your mother."

I finally decided to do my science project on how temperature changes the stickiness of different kinds of tape. It was fun because I got to blow a hairdryer at the tape to make it hot. I tried putting ice on it to make it cold, but the tape kept getting wet, so I ended up just putting it in the freezer.

Doing the experiment was the easy part, though. The science journal and the display were another story.

I sat at the kitchen table with the journal open. I had written one single thing: "Is Tape Stickier When It's Hot or When It's Cold?" And then I'd gotten bored and drawn pictures of little bugs stuck to a piece of tape trying to get off.

I got more and more frustrated as I stared at the journal. I started tipping my chair back and then slamming the legs down on the floor. I did it harder and harder and faster and faster, until Mom ran into the room.

"Jay Jay! What's wrong?" she asked.

"I can't do this!" I shouted at her. "I have ADHD and so I can't do this! I'll never be able to do anything right!"

Mom took a big breath, and I could tell she was trying not to yell right back at me. She made me come in the living room with her, and we sat down on the couch together. I was still upset, so I started punch-

ing the back of the couch. We just sat there for a few minutes, me punching the couch and Mom looking at me.

Finally, I said, "It's not my fault I have ADHD! Why do I keep getting in trouble for something that's not my fault?"

"It is hard," Mom said. "Everybody has something different they have to deal with, and for you, it's ADHD. But you can't use it as an excuse not to do your best. It's your life, and good or bad, you are the one who has to live it. Making excuses just hurts yourself. No, it's not fair, and it's not your fault. It's not anybody's fault. But I—and Dr. Kelley, your teachers, and the principal—will do everything we can to help you deal with it. That doesn't mean letting you do less work or sloppy work. It means things like the schedule—which I think has helped a little, even if you don't want to admit it—and probably taking some medicine that will help you be able to focus."

Dr. Kelley had said something to Mom about medicine at our first appointment, but she had also said she wanted to wait and see how I did with more structure first. Since more structure had only helped a little, she agreed now that I should start taking medicine for the ADHD.

I didn't like the medicine. It made me feel like I was sick or something, having to take a pill. But after just one day, Mrs. Harris said, "Good job today, Jay Jay." Suddenly, I realized that I'd pretty much sat still and paid attention all day.

I still didn't like taking medicine, though.

"Mom, does having ADHD mean I can't ever do anything cool or important?" I asked that evening. "Do you think I'll just have to sit around taking pills and following a schedule my whole life?"

"Are you kidding me?" Mom asked. "Do you know how many famous people have ADHD? Why don't you look it up on the Internet and see?"

So I looked it up. Mostly, they were a bunch of people I'd never heard of, but then I saw a name I knew—Michael Phelps.

"Mom, Mom!" I yelled. "Michael Phelps has ADHD too! And he's won the most gold medals ever!"

"See," Mom said. "Sky's the limit."

When the day of the Science Fair came, my project was ready. My journal was done and everything. Okay, so it was still a little messy, and there were still drawings on every other page, but it was done.

I set up my project in the gym with all the other kids and then stood next to it as a bunch of teachers and parents walked around and looked at everything.

Mr. Martinez came by and stopped next to my project. "This is a really good job, Jay Jay," he said. "I'm very proud of you."

Then Mrs. Harris stopped and smiled at me. "This is wonderful, Jay Jay. You have the makings of a great scientist."

I was starting to feel pretty good. Like maybe ADHD wasn't the end of the world, and maybe I would be able to do something cool with my life after all.

I lay in bed that night and looked at the new poster of Michael Phelps that Mom had bought me. I smiled as I started to fall asleep. *Sky's the limit,* I thought.

Kids and ADHD

Nearly one out of twenty children has attention-deficit hyperactivity disorder—ADHD. That means that at least one kid in every classroom probably has ADHD. ADHD makes it hard for that kid to pay attention, stay *focused*, and control his behavior.

Kids with ADHD might have a hard time sitting still in class, focusing on a homework assignment without getting *distracted*, or remembering all the steps to solve a tough math problem. This can make school difficult. It can make it harder to learn new material and remember lessons they have already

If you are focused, you are concentrating on something.

A person who is distracted is having trouble paying attention.

learned. It can get in the way of their life at home with their family, and it will be a part of how they get along with friends and family.

Kids with ADHD have a hard time focusing on their schoolwork, becoming distracted easily.

All this isn't the fault of the person with ADHD. Children with ADHD aren't simply messy or lazy or less hard-working. They're not "bad" or "naughty," even though their behaviors may seem that way. In fact, many kids with ADHD have to work harder to cope with the same homework and the same *issues* at home that other kids handle more easily. Kids with ADHD can grow up to be just as successful as those who don't have ADHD, but they also have special *challenges*.

Issues are personal problems.

Challenges are things you find difficult.

What Are the Symptoms of ADHD?

Everyone gets distracted from time to time. That's natural and to be expected—and not everyone who gets distracted or fidgets in class has ADHD. But if a child feels distracted a lot of the time—and it ends up hurting her schoolwork, friendships, or family relationships—she might be showing symptoms of ADHD.

ADHD can make keeping track of many different thoughts at once a challenge.

In order to be *diagnosed* with ADHD, a child must show these *symptoms* before he is seven years old and for more than six months. The child must have ADHD-type behaviors more often than other kids the same age do, and these behaviors must hurt his ability to do well in school, and interact with kids his age or at home. He must be having trouble in two of these areas (at home, at school, or with other kids his age) before he can be said to have ADHD.

ADHD symptoms fall into three groups: *inattention*, *hyperactivity*, and *impulsivity*. To be diagnosed with ADHD, a child must show six symptoms from the hyperactivity or impulsivity groups, six from the inattention group, or six symptoms from inattention and six from the hyperactivity/impulsivity groups. It is most common for kids to be diagnosed with this last combined form of ADHD.

When someone is *diagnosed*, that means a doctor has found out what is wrong with him.

Symptoms are signs of a sickness or disease.

Inattention is when a person is not paying attention.

Hyperactivity is being more excited or energetic than is normal.

Impulsivity is when a person feels sudden urges to do things.

Signs of Inattention

- getting distracted easily, missing small **details**, and being forgetful

> **Details** *are little parts of something.*

- jumping back and forth between many activities at once and having a hard time focusing on a single thing
- becoming bored easily
- having a hard time finishing something or starting something new
- daydreaming, not listening, or having a hard time understanding a lot of information at once
- having a hard time following directions

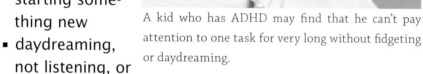

A kid who has ADHD may find that he can't pay attention to one task for very long without fidgeting or daydreaming.

Signs of Hyperactivity

- talking nonstop
- having a hard time sitting quietly for very long
- having a hard time doing quiet things that don't take much energy
- constantly moving around

Signs of Impulsivity

- speaking or acting without thinking
- having a hard time waiting for anything
- interrupting conversations or activities
- becoming impatient easily

Diagnosing ADHD

ADHD is most often diagnosed between the ages of three and eight. An early diagnosis is important for kids with ADHD, because it's the first step to getting the help these kids need from doctors, teachers, and parents.

Sometimes, though, it's hard to tell the difference between "normal kid behavior" and ADHD symptoms. For example, all little kids get distracted easily and most young children have lots of energy. This makes it hard to diagnose ADHD. Another thing that can make it

Kids who get a diagnosis for ADHD earlier in their lives have more time to learn skills that can help them succeed with ADHD.

hard to diagnose ADHD is that since each child is different, each child may have different ADHD symptoms. This means that no test can be used by itself to diagnose ADHD. Doctors and **specialists** must also make sure that they don't confuse symptoms of another illness or health problem with the symptoms of attention-deficit disorder.

Sometimes children with ADHD are diagnosed by **pediatricians**, but a **psychiatrist**, **psychologist**, or other mental health specialist can also diagnose the disorder.

Before a child can be diagnosed with ADHD, doctors and specialists must rule out problems with seeing or hearing, **learning disabilities**,

Specialists are people who are trained to be very good at one particular thing.

Pediatricians are doctors who treat children.

A **psychiatrist** is a special doctor who treats problems with people's minds or emotions.

A **psychologist** studies how the mind works and helps people handle their emotions.

Learning disabilities are problems within a person's brain that makes learning certain things—such as reading—more difficult than it is for other people.

or *emotional problems*. For example, maybe a child isn't paying attention in school because she can't see the whiteboard. Maybe she can see the board, but she can't read the letters that are written there. If that's the case, she may feel bored in class, and have a hard time paying attention. Or a child who is depressed because of a problem at home might also show symptoms that are similar to those of ADHD. Once specialists make sure that no other sickness or disorder is causing the child's symptoms and everything points to ADHD, then the diagnosis will be made.

Emotional problems make it difficult for a person to cope with her feelings, and may make it hard for her to handle ordinary life.

Genes are tiny codes inside cells that determine what a person looks like and what problems he has. These "codes" are passed along from parents to their children.

What Causes ADHD?

Scientists have many ideas about what causes ADHD, but they don't agree on any one thing that causes the disorder. Most scientists believe that ADHD is caused by more than one thing. Studies have shown that *genes* may be one cause, but scientists are also looking into whether other things—such as diet or *environment*—help to cause ADHD.

Genes

We inherit our genes from our parents and then pass them on to our children. Scientists are busy studying specific genes that may make people more or less likely to develop ADHD. As they learn more about the genes that may be involved in ADHD, *researchers* and scientists can learn more about how to treat ADHD, or how to stop its symptoms altogether.

Doctors and scientists don't know what exactly causes ADHD, but they are still searching for answers.

Your environment is everything surrounding you, including your home, your family, your diet, your friends, your school, and the outdoors.

Researchers are people who do experiments and study the results.

Environment

Researchers think that cigarette smoking and using alcohol during pregnancy may help cause ADHD in children.

Young children who are around *lead* may also have a higher risk of having ADHD.

Some people believe that *food additives* (for example, food coloring and *preservatives*) can cause hyperactivity symptoms in children. Many scientists disagree with this, however. Research on food additives and ADHD have shown that only five percent of children (five kids out of a hundred) with ADHD are helped by changing diet or limiting food additives.

Lead is a chemical sometimes found in old paint and drinking water.

Food additives are chemicals added to food to make it look or taste better.

Preservatives are chemicals added to food to keep it from spoiling.

Brain Injuries

Children whose brains have been hurt somehow often have some of the symptoms of ADHD, but doctors usually think of this as a different condition from ADHD.

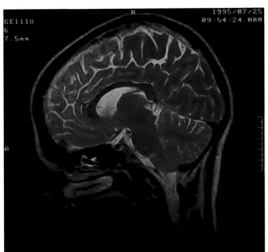

Some types of brain injuries can cause symptoms that may seem like ADHD.

What DOESN'T Cause ADHD?

Most scientists agree that ADHD is not caused by:

- too much sugar
- too much TV
- poor home life
- poor schools
- bad parents

Treating ADHD

Though ADHD has no cure, the disorder can be treated with medicine, *therapy*, changes in behavior, or a combination of several methods.

Therapy tries to solve problems by talking with a mental health expert such as a counselor or psychologist.

Medicine

ADHD is often treated with a type of medicine called a stimulant. Stimulants can calm hyperactive or impulsive children, and help them focus. Many types of stimulants are used to treat ADHD. Because each child with ADHD has different symptom, doctors must find the medicine that works best for each child. Stimulants can come in the form of pills, liquids, or capsules.

Many kids will take one pill in the morning that lasts all day. Parents and doctors decide when the child needs the medication most (for school or for special activities, for example) and when he can go without it.

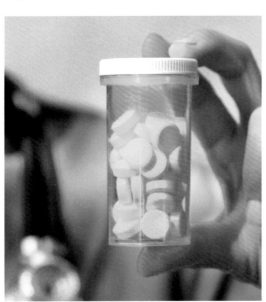

Side effects are unwanted things a medicine causes, besides treating the problem it is supposed to solve.

The medicines kids take for ADHD are very safe, but they need to be taken exactly as the doctor says is best. Some of these medicines do have *side effects*, such as making it hard for a kid to fall sleep or making him not feel very hungry. Side effects that one child has might not be a problem for someone else. The right medication is different for every child, and kids may not react the same way to the same medicine.

No medicine can cure ADHD, but often medicine can help a child handle school, family, and friends better—but it's not the only way to treat ADHD.

Medicines can help kids with ADHD focus on work and pay attention in class.

Therapy

ADHD can also be treated through therapy, or a combination of therapy and medication. Therapy often means teaching new skills to kids with ADHD and their families. Sometimes, simple *strategies* can make a big difference.

For instance, a *behavioral therapist* can help a child change the way he deals with the symptoms of ADHD. Behavioral therapy might mean teaching a kid to organize his life better, or teaching him to understand his feelings. Even small things like making to-do lists, setting *routines*, or splitting large jobs into several smaller ones can help kids handle the challenges of ADHD. Therapy can also help children with ADHD learn *social skills* such as how to wait their turn, how to talk about their feelings more clearly and calmly, and how to think before speaking.

Strategies are different plans to solve a problem.

A behavioral therapist is a psychologist who helps people change the way they act.

Routines are when you do things the same way every day.

Social skills are needed to get along with other people.

The child with ADHD might attend therapy with her parents and brothers and sisters, so the whole family can learn ways to work together to handle ADHD. Parents are especially important for helping a child with ADHD do better at home and school. A parent's praise, understanding, and support can make a big difference in the life of a child with ADHD. Parents can also help build routines for the entire family that will help the child with ADHD cope better. Family therapy can also help kids and their parents learn new ways to talk about their frustrations and other feelings.

ADHD in School

ADHD can make school a challenge, but there are many ways that a child can get help if he needs it. Teachers and other school staff can help a student with ADHD be more organized, which will help him be more successful in school. These things might seem small, but they can make a big difference in the life of a kid with ADHD.

Scheduling

Routines at school are important for children with ADHD. Having a daily schedule—a plan that tells a child exactly what time to

A schedule of all homework can help kids with ADHD keep up with assignments and hand projects in on time.

expect something to happen every day—can give structure to the day and keep a kid with ADHD focused on one thing at a time.

School Assignments

It can be tough for kids with ADHD to keep track of everything that's expected of them at school. By using a notebook to write down homework assignments, children with ADHD can more easily remember a task and make sure they complete it.

A Place for Everything

Keeping things neat can be a key to success for kids with ADHD. For instance, organizing cubbies, desks, and lockers at school can help a child remember what he needs to bring to each class. Color-coding notebooks and textbooks can also help.

Other Things That Help

One-on-one tutoring can help many students with ADHD. Even something as simple as sitting closer to the front of the classroom can change the way a child with ADHD learns. Many schools have special programs for children with ADHD. U.S. law guarantees that children who have special needs for learning get the education they need to learn.

ADHD and Special Education

Not all kids with ADHD need *special education*, but some do. A law known as the Individuals with Disabilities Education Act, or IDEA, describes how schools decide which kids need special education. In order to *qualify* for IDEA, the child's condition must get in the way of him learning or taking part in school activities.

The IDEA law lists thirteen different kinds of *disabilities* that may mean a child will

Special education teaches kids who have trouble learning because of some disability.

To qualify means to fit the definition of something or to meet the requirements.

Disabilities are problems—either physical or mental—that get in the way of a person doing what other people can do.

Some kids with ADHD may get one-on-one help from a teacher or tutor.

40

need special education. ADHD falls under a *category* in IDEA called "Other Health Impairment."

The law requires that:

- the child has problems performing well at school activities.
- the child's parent, teacher, or other school staff person must ask that the child be examined for a disability.

> A *category* is a group or a certain kind of thing.
>
> When something is *evaluated*, it is examined to see in which category it belongs.

- the child is *evaluated* to decide if she does indeed have a disability and to figure out what kind of special education she needs.
- a group of people, including the kid's parents, teachers, and a school psychologist, meets to decide on a plan for helping him (or her). This plan is called an Individualized Education Program (IEP). The IEP spells out exactly what the child needs in order to succeed at school.

Growing Up with ADHD

ADHD is usually diagnosed in young children, but it doesn't go away as kids grow older. As kids become teens, they may learn to cope better, though. Sometimes, they can become less hyperactive, but they will probably still have to work at sticking to one task at a time.

Parents often have less control over teenagers' lives, so kids with ADHD may not always stick to their treatments as they grow up—but teens with ADHD may still need medicine to help them handle their symptoms. They can still benefit from clear rules at home. They do better with schedules that stay the same from day to day, and they need to find ways to keep their belongings organized. Keeping treatments in place—or changing them to suit the needs of each individual—is important as kids with ADHD get older.

Adults have ADHD, too. Like kids and teens with ADHD, they can use a few different methods to handle their symptoms, including medicine and therapy. Some adults might have ADHD and not know it. When these adults were children, people didn't know as much about ADHD as people do today, and now that they're grown up, these individuals may not understand why they have so many problems handling some of life's challenges. In a way, the children who grow up knowing they have ADHD are lucky. They will learn to cope with their symptoms better than those who are diagnosed later in life.

Learning More

Every year, scientists and doctors understand more about what causes ADHD. They also learn new ways to help children with ADHD. Scientists and researchers learn more about ADHD by studying the brain, the environment, and children's behavior. As doctors and scientists understand more about ADHD, schools and teachers can help kids with ADHD learn better. Families can help these children be happier at home.

Having ADHD can be hard for a child and his family to handle. If you have ADHD—or if you know someone with ADHD—you may find some of the symptoms frustrating or annoying. But in the long run, kids with ADHD aren't so different from those who do not

> *Someone who is **considerate** does things that are good for other people, not just for herself.*
>
> *A **respectful** person is polite and courteous to everyone.*

have ADHD. Kids with ADHD get their feelings hurt, they feel proud when they do a good job, they can be good friends, and they love their families—just like any kid. If someone in your class has ADHD, understand that he might finish tasks differently, forget something, or make a mistake sometimes. But we all make mistakes, and we all have different challenges that we face. By being *considerate* and *respectful* to everyone, we can create a better world for us all—at school, at home, with our friends.

Further Reading

Association for Youth, Children and Natural Psychology. *Overcoming Attention Deficit Hyperactivity Disorder (ADHD) without Medication: A Parent's and Educator Guidebook.* Newark, N. J.: Association for Youth, Children and Natural Psychology, 2009.

Barkley, R. A. *Taking Charge of ADHD: The Complete, Authoritative Guide for Parents.* New York: Guilford Press, 2000.

Dawson, P. and R. Guare. *Smart but Scattered: The Revolutionary "Executive Skills" Approach to Helping Kids Reach Their Potential.* New York: Guilford Press, 2009.

DeRuvo, S. L. *Strategies for Teaching Adolescents with ADHD: Effective Classroom Techniques Across the Content Areas, Grades 6-12.* San Francisco, Calif.: John Wiley & Sons, 2009.

Hart, A. and R. K. Debroitner. *Moving Beyond ADD/ADHD, Second Edition.* Kill Devil Hills, N. C. Transpersonal Publishing, 2007.

Honos-Webb, L. *The Gift of ADHD Activity Book: 101 Ways to Turn Your Child's Problems into Strengths.* Oakland, Calif.: New Harbinger Publications, 2007.

Kutscher, M. L. *Kids in the Syndrome Mix of ADHD, LD, Asperger's, Tourette's Bipolar and More!: The One Stop Guide for Parents, Teachers and Other Professionals.* London: Jessica Kingsley Publishers, 2005.

Lougy, R. A. *Teaching Young Children with ADHD: Successful Strategies and Practical Interventions for PreK-3.* Thousand Oaks, Calif.: Corwin Press, 2007.

McIntyre, T. *The Behavioral Survival Guide for Kids: How to Make Good Choices and Stay Out of Trouble.* Minneapolis, Minn.: Free Spirit Publishing, 2003.

Mooney, J. and D. Cole. *Learning Outside the Lines: Two Ivy League Students with Learning Disabilities and ADHD Give You the Tools.* New York: Fireside, 2000.

Parker, H. C. *Problem Solver Guide for Students with ADHD: Ready-to-Use Interventions for Elementary and Secondary Students.* Plantation, Fla.: Specialty Press, 2000.

Power, T. J., Karustis, J. L., and D. F. Habboushe. *Homework Success for Children with ADHD: A Family-School Intervention Program.* New York: Guilford Press, 2001.

Steer, J. and K. Horstmann. *Helping Kids and Teens with ADHD in School: A Workbook for Classroom Support and Managing Transitions.* London: Jessica Kingsley Publishers, 2009.

Taylor, J. F. *The Survival Guide for Kids with ADD or ADHD.* Minneapolis, Minn.: Free Spirit Publishing, 2006.

Wilens, T. E.. *Straight Talk about Psychiatric Medications for Kids, Third Edition.* New York: Guilford Press, 2009.

Find Out More On the Internet

All Kinds of Minds
www.allkindsofminds.org

Attention Deficit Information Network
www.addinfonetwork.com

Center for Mental Health Services
mentalhealth.samhsa.gov/cmhs

CHADD (Children and Adults with Attention Deficit Disorder)
www.chadd.org

Council for Exceptional Children
www.cec.sped.org

Federation of Families for Children's Mental Health
ffcmh.org

Mental Health Net
adhd.mentalhelp.net

The National Attention Deficit Disorder Association
www.add.org

National Information Center for Children and Youth with Disabilities (NICHCY)
www.nichcy.org

Disclaimer

The websites listed on this page were active at the time of publication. The publisher is not responsible for websites that have changed their address or discontinued operation since the date of publication. The publisher will review and update the websites upon each reprint.

Index

About the Authors

Sheila Stewart has written several dozen books for young people, both fiction and nonfiction, although she especially enjoys writing fiction. She has a master's degree in English and now works as a writer and editor. She lives with her two children in a house overflowing with books, in the Southern Tier of New York State.

Camden Flath is a writer living and working in Binghamton, New York. He has a degree in English and has written several books for young people. He is interested in current political, social, and economic issues and applies those interests to his writing.

About the Consultant

Dr. Carolyn Bridgemohan is board certified in developmental behavioral pediatrics and practices at the Developmental Medicine Center at Children's Hospital Boston. She is the director of the Autism Care Program and an assistant professor at Harvard Medical School. Her specialty areas are autism and other pervasive developmental disorders, developmental and learning problems, and developmental and behavioral pediatrics.